ACQUISITION OF CUBA.

SPEECH

OF

HON. ZACHARIAH CHANDLER,

OF MICHIGAN,

IN THE SENATE OF THE UNITED STATES, FEBRUARY 17, 1859.

The Senate having resumed the consideration of the bill making appropriation to facilitate the acquisition of Cuba by negotiation—

Mr. CHANDLER said:

Mr. PRESIDENT: This is a most extraordinary proposition to be presented to the Congress of the United States, at this time. With a Treasury bankrupt, and the Government borrowing money to pay its daily expenses, and no efficient remedy proposed for that state of things; with your great national works in the Northwest going to decay, and no money to repair them; without harbors of refuge for your commerce, and no money to erect them; with a national debt of $70,000,000 which is increasing in a time of profound peace at the rate of $30,000,000 per annum, the Senate of the United States is startled by a proposition to borrow $30,000,000. And for what, sir? To pay just claims against this Government, which have been long deferred? No, sir; you have no money for any such purpose as that. Is it to repair your national works on the northwestern lakes, to repair your harbors, to rebuild your light-houses? No, sir; you have no money for that. Is it to build a railroad to the Pacific, connecting the eastern and western slopes of this continent by bands of iron, and opening up the vast interior of the continent to settlement? No, sir; you say that is unconstitutional. What, then, do you propose to do with this $30,000,000? Is it to purchase the Island of Cuba? No, sir; for you are already advised in advance that Spain will not sell the island. More, sir; you are advised in advance that she will take a proposition for its purchase as a national insult, to be rejected with scorn and contempt. The action of her Cortes and of her Government, on the reception of the President's message, proves this beyond all controversy.

What, then, I ask again, do you propose to do with this $30,000,000? I ask any friend of the measure what he proposes to do with the money? The question is absurd. There is no man, woman, or child, who does not know for what purpose this $30,000,000 is intended. It is a great corruption fund for bribery, and for bribery only. It is a proposition worthy of its author; it is a proposition worthy of the writer of the Ostend manifesto; a proposition worthy of the brigand; worthy of James Buchanan; but it is unworthy of the President of the United States; it is a proposition disgraceful to be made to the Congress of the United States.

Again I ask, what do you propose to do with the money? Is it intended that this grand corruption fund shall be used in the purchase of foreign ministers and ministers of State and high Spanish officials? Is this what the friends of the measure would have us believe it to be? Such, possibly, a small portion of it may be intended for; but, in my estimation, that portion will be found to be infinitesimally small. There are other, and, in the estimation of some, more important, objects to be attained by the use of this money.

The Democratic party is damaged, badly damaged at the North. Its principles are gone, and even its occupation of public plunder is gone, for there is nothing left to steal; your Treasury is bankrupt, and there is no hope of replenishing it before the presidential contest of 1860. In this emergency something must be done for the Democratic party, and here is the proposition to do it. A new issue is to be raised to call off the attention of the country from past extravagant expenditures and present bankruptcy. Cuba is to be the cry in the next presidential election, and $30,000,000 is to be the inducement to cry loud and long. This is a mere clap-trap proposition to go into the canvass of 1860; and the friends of this measure have no more idea of purchasing Cuba under it than I have of buying it on private account. They are to go before the country upon this cry of Cuba, and upon it they hope to float into power again in 1860. Vain, fallacious hope. Forty Cubas and $300,000,000 as a bribery and corruption fund, would not save the Democratic party from that annihilation which the Almighty has decreed.

But, sir, let us examine this proposition in its practical effects upon our constituency. I propose to take a practical view of it. I propose, before we go into a speculation of this kind, to ascertain whether it will pay. The computation which I am about to present, was made before Oregon was admitted, which has one member of the House of Representatives, and this fact would vary my figures a few dollars; but a few dollars only. Of this $30,000,000 bribery fund, each congressional district will pay $127,118 64. The State of Michigan, under the present representation, according to the census of 1850, having four members, will pay $508,474 56. But the population of Michigan has more than doubled since 1850, and she is now entitled, according to her population, to eight Representatives; and will, in 1860, be entitled to eight, at a ratio of one hundred and twenty-five thousand people to a Representative; so that her present proportion would be, according to a proper apportionment, $1,016,949 12, the interest upon which, at six per cent. per annum, would be $61,016 94. I name six per cent., because if you go into any such wild scheme as this, borrowing money to buy islands, you will find your national credit below par, according to the present rate of interest; and I believe six per cent. is the lowest rate at which you can borrow money if you conclude to go into this fillibustering proposition for the campaign of 1860. I say, then, you propose to mortgage my State of Michigan for $1,016,949, and to compel her people to pay an annual tax of $61,016. Before I vote this mortgage, and this perpetual annual tax upon the people of Michigan, I desire to consult my constituents; and after I have consulted them, even if they should make up their minds that this was a wise scheme, I should tell them that upon that point I differ from them.

But, sir, this is not all. You propose to authorize the President to purchase the Island of Cuba for any price he may see fit. It is true the Senator from Ohio, [Mr. PUGH,] has offered an amendment placing a limit on the price, but it has not been adopted, and if it were I do not suppose it would have any effect on the negotiation. What would President Buchanan care for $50,000,000, more or less, to accomplish his darling scheme? Give him this $30,000,000 to start with and he will pay two hundred, or two hundred and fifty, or any other number of millions that it may suit his whim to pay. I care not for your limit—he will not regard it. I will, however, take as the basis of my calculation the lowest price named as the sum which Spain will consent to accept for Cuba; to wit: $200,000,000. Two hundred million seems to be considered, on all hands, as the minimum price. What the maximum may be, I know not. I take as the basis of my calculation the minimum of $200,000,000. If that be the amount, each congressional district in the United States would pay $847,454, and the State of Michigan, as at present represented under the census of 1850, would pay $3,389,816; but, as I have already stated, her population has more than doubled since the last census, and is rapidly increasing, so that her present proportion would be $6,779,632. Upon this sum the annual perpetual interest would be $406,777 92. I call it perpetual, for no sane man believes that, if this debt be created, it will ever be paid in the world. It is but the commencement of an irredeemable debt. I say, then, you propose to mortgage the State of Michigan for $6,779,632, and to compel her to pay a perpetual annual tax of $406,777 92.

Sir, before I vote for any such scheme as that, I want authority from home; and I advise the Senator from Ohio to listen to his constituents before he votes for any such scheme. My word for it, if he has not heard from them, he will in 1861.

Mr. PUGH. I will take care of my constituents; let the Senator take care of his own.

Mr. CHANDLER. The State of Ohio will have to pay, of this purchase money, $17,896,534, the perpetual annual tax of which, on that State, will be $1,073,791. Of the $30,000,000 appropriated by this bill, Ohio will pay $2,669,478, the annual interest on which, at six per cent., will be $160,168. The Senator says he will take care of that. I trust he will; and I can assure him that if he does not, the people of Ohio will.

Now, let us admit for the sake of the argument, that this proposition is brought forward in good faith and will be successfully terminated, what does the State of Michigan gain, what does the State of Ohio gain, what do any of the northwestern States gain by the purchase of the Island of Cuba? I know something of Cuba, something of its soil, something of its climate, something of its people, their manners and customs, something of their religion, something of their crimes. I spent a winter in the interior of the Island of Cuba a few years since, and can therefore speak from personal knowledge. I differ in my views from the honorable Senator from Louisiana, [Mr. BENJAMIN.] My personal observation does not accord with his theories. Much of the soil of the island is rich and exceedingly productive; but it is in no way comparable to the prairies and bottom-lands of the Great West. You can go into almost any of your Territories and select an equal number of acres and you will have a more valuable State than you can possibly make out of Cuba. You have hundreds of millions of acres of land to which you can extinguish the Indian title for a song, and obtain better lands and create better States than you will ever make out of Cuba.

The Island of Cuba contains nineteen million three hundred and fifty thousand acres, and you propose to pay for it $200,000,000; or in other words, you propose to pay for the Island of Cuba more than ten dollars an acre for every acre of land on it, and then you do not acquire an acre. You are selling infinitely better lands, and have millions upon millions of them, for $1 25; and yet you propose to tax the people of the United States to pay ten dollars an acre for land that you do not get when you pay the money.

I notice by the report of the honorable Senator from Louisiana, [Mr. SLIDELL,] that Cuba contains, at this time, a population of one million nine thousand and sixty inhabitants, including negroes, old men, and small children. You propose to pay nearly two hundred dollars a head for every man, woman, child, and negro on the island, and then you do not own one of them. You propose to pay $200,000,000—for what? For the right to govern one million of the refuse of the earth. You propose to pay $200,000,000 to bring in a population that you would reject with scorn if they were now to apply for admission into the Union, free of all expense.

Do you think that proposition will pay? Do

you think it will commend itself to the people of the Northwest? Do you think it will commend itself to the people of this Union? What do you get after you pay your $200,000,000? You acquire the right to build fortifications; to send an army to Cuba; to govern it; to create a navy to protect it; to expend through all time, from twenty-five to a hundred millions per annum, to take care of it. That is all you get. Do you think it will pay? But, as I said before, I know something of the people of this island, and something of their manners and customs.

The white population consists chiefly of creoles, or native-born Cubans. Of the slave population I should think a large majority are native-born Africans. The honorable Senator from Louisiana [Mr. BENJAMIN] spoke the other day of the great mortality among the slaves of Cuba. If he meant to apply his remarks on that point to the creole slaves, he made a vast mistake; for I never in my life saw a more healthy set of persons than the creole slaves of Cuba. They are not half so hard worked, they are better fed, they live longer than the slaves of Louisiana; and they are not as cruelly treated. This remark was made to me over and over again, "Give me anything but a Yankee master." They do not want an American master. He is energetic, he drives, he works his negroes; but the creoles are so utterly indolent themselves, that they allow their negroes to do pretty much what they please. If the Senator meant his remark to apply to the Africans, it was, perhaps correct. At the time I was upon the island, the mortality of the native Africans was estimated thus: one fifth of all shipped from the coast of Africa died upon the passage; one fifth more committed suicide within the first year after they were landed on the island; one fifth more died the first year in the process of acclimation, because they were unaccustomed to toil, unaccustomed to that mode of living. Consequently, three fifths of the entire exportation from the coast of Africa were lost in one year from the date of their exportation. In regard to the remaining two fifths, however, after becoming acclimated, they live as long as creole negroes. It will be seen that three fifths being destroyed the first year, in order to get an average of any length of time, you must rate a long life to the rest, unless you shorten the duration, perhaps to the time the Senator mentioned; but the lives of the creole negroes are as long as those of any other people in the world.

Now, as to the white population: they are ignorant, vicious, and priest-ridden. Prior to the administration of General Tacon, there was not a crime on the calendar which had not its fixed value in the Island of Cuba. I had at one time the tariff of crime there, but at the present moment I only recollect a single item. The price of assassination was two ounces of gold, or thirty-four dollars a head! You could have any man assassinated for thirty-four dollars before the administration of Tacon; and I was informed by many old Cubans you could scarcely walk out in the streets of Havana in the morning without finding one or more dead bodies, the result of the last night's assassinations and robberies. My own experience is, that the gibbet was a common sight—the gibbet, with the human skull rattling in the wind, at the corner of four roads, or at some place where a crime had been committed and the murderer met his fate.

On the accession of Tacon to office, he increased the army to twenty thousand men, and did establish, as the honorable Senator from Louisiana [Mr. BENJAMIN] said, an absolute military despotism, which exists there to this day. But it was not as the Senator said to prevent insurrection; it was to prevent crime, and that only; and if that military despotism had not been established, and had not been ruled with an iron hand, Cuba would be to-day what it was before the administration of Tacon. As I said before, the people are ignorant and vicious. They will not labor, and they will resort to any shifts of crime to obtain subsistence. Bribery is universal, from the Governor General, who receives two ounces of gold per head for every slave landed on the island. Let a slave trader land a single negro without paying his two ounces of gold, that negro will be wrested from him within three days. Two ounces of gold per head is the regular established bribe for every slave landed on the Island of Cuba, and it is done as publicly as almost any other transaction there. I went into the barracoons at Havana, and saw eleven hundred slaves within three days from the time of their landing there from the coast of Africa. They were landed within ten miles of the Moro Castle, and marched directly up to Havana, and placed in the barracoons for sale publicly, under the very eye of the Captain General. Everybody was talking about it, and the ship that brought them over, lay as quietly in the harbor of Havana as any merchant ship. If you had seen, as I did, those eleven hundred miserable wretches, you would not be surprised at the mortality among them. The laws of Spain are to-day as severe against the slave trade as those of the United States; nevertheless, slaves are continually imported there, and it is done because the Captain General is bribed. It is a well known fact, that every Captain General of Cuba acquires an immense fortune in two or three years, and it is from the slave trade and that alone. From the judge on the bench, from the priest in the pulpit, to the lowest tide-waiter, bribery is the rule, and there are no exceptions. You cannot remove the dead body of your friend from the Island of Cuba without bribing the priest, bribing the captain of the Partero, bribing the judge, and bribing the custom-house officer, through whose hand it passes. I know that, because I have had to pay the bribes.

Is not this a beautiful population to bring into the Union as a State—a beautiful population to take rank with the old States of this Union? But, sir, that is not all. The Catholic religion rules supreme in the Island of Cuba; no other religion is tolerated. Even the rites of a Christian burial are denied to a Protestant upon that island. The people are superstitious and vicious; and they are bigots as well. They are devout Catholics. The Catholic Church is true to Spain; the Catholic Church is true to despotism; and the people there, to a man, are true to the Church. If the honorable Senator from Louisiana has seen hundreds, or if he has seen one hundred, Cubans who were panting for liberty, as he asserts, he has seen every one that that island produced. There are a few creole Cubans, who have been educated in the United States, that are intelligent, that care nothing about their church, who are anxious to get their hands into the Treasury. They are anxious for plunder; they are anxious for positions where they can receive bribes. True patriotism does not exist on the Island of Cuba. They love the very chains that bind them. They love their church; they love this very military despotism of which complaint is made. The men of whom the Senator from Louisiana speaks, are men the majority of whom have been banished from the island. Where was the declaration of independence which he brought before us written? Who wrote it? Where was it adopted? In my opinion, it was adopted in some tavern in New Orleans. The people of Cuba never adopted a declaration of independence. What was the fate of the gallant Crittenden when he went to Cuba to help to rescue them from oppression? What became of that young man and the fifty associates who were with him, when they went there with arms in their hands prepared to shed their blood for the redemption of the Island of Cuba? Where, then, were the patriots who were thirsting for freedom? If there was one on the island, he kept himself pretty well out of sight; and that gallant young man, ten minutes before he suffered death, wrote a letter to a friend in the United States, saying: "I did not come here to plunder; I came here in good faith to aid these people in acquiring their freedom; I supposed they were thirsting for liberty; but I have been deceived. My time has come." In a postscript he added: "I will die like a man."

Where were the liberty-thirsting Cubans then, when as gallant a soul as ever lived on the face of this earth went to his last account because he sympathized with "gallant, suffering" Cubans? Sir, the gallantry is not there. There is no such thing as a love of liberty there. Do you want these people in your Union? Are you prepared to pay $200,000,000 to bring such a set of criminals into this Union? Do you propose to keep an army of twenty thousand men in a climate where they will be decimated every year, to govern that island? That is what Spain has to do, and that is what you will have to do if you mean to keep the people from cutting each other's throats. You will have to keep up a navy there to protect your possession, if you get it. You must spend from fifteen to twenty million dollars a year to govern the island; and in addition to that, you propose to place a perpetual annual tax of $12,000,000 upon the people of the United States for the purchase. I ask Senators whether they consider that a game that will pay?

Suppose you get the island: what will you do with it? Your people cannot live there. The impression has gone abroad that in the interior of the Island of Cuba the climate is cool and healthy; but such is not the fact. Tropical diseases always rage there at certain seasons of the year, and the foreign population is usually decimated every year. You cannot even sleep on a mattress, during the winter, on that island. The heat is so intense that you are obliged to forego the luxury of a mattress, and sleep in a hammock or upon canvas. Besides, there are certain other luxuries that I wish to call to the attention of northern men who may propose to go there. You are compelled to sleep under mosquito bars all the year round; and if you do not find scorpions in your boots in the morning, you will be more fortunate than I was. Lizards run about in every direction; worms annoy you at every turn. This is a beautiful place to emigrate to! And yet you propose to pay $200,000,000 for the island. In my opinion, it is not a paying investment.

But, sir, as I said before, this bill is not to buy the Island of Cuba, for you are advised in advance that you cannot get it. This is a mere electioneering scheme for 1860. It is to be one of the planks in the Democratic platform in 1860; and I propose very briefly to review a certain other plank which you have in that platform, as it has only two left—this one is not yet in. You have destroyed all your old platforms; they are utterly annihilated. Even the Cincinnati platform of tender years has ceased to be; and I am not surprised that that platform has been destroyed. There never was a sound plank in it. It said that everything was left "perfectly free, subject to the Constitution of the United States;" but the knowing ones in that convention were perfectly aware at that time that the Constitution of the United States was virtually subverted by a decision which the Supreme Court dared not then make, and whose final enunciation depended upon the result of that election. If President Buchanan had not been elected, the Dred Scott decision would not have been made. I propose now to spend a very little time in examining this last new platform of the Democratic party. The Supreme Court of the United States was merciful in its work of destruction. The Cincinnati platform was built precisely as boys build cob-houses—to see who could first knock them down; and the missile which the Supreme Court threw at the Cincinnati platform, which destroyed it, and which will virtually overturn the Constitution of the United States when it becomes the law; that very missile was itself a Democratic platform, which the Democratic leaders made great haste to mount; and at the North they found it large enough. There was but one plank to it, but it would hold all the Democratic party there. They had become infinitesimally small and few in number before that last new platform, and are growing beautifully less day by day.

I insist that the Dred Scott decision—for it is needless for me to say that it is to that I allude—is the only Democratic platform that now exists; and if any man throughout this broad land, who holds a Government office of any value whatever, doubts it, let him try the experiment. Let him say that he does not consider the Dred Scott decision the Democratic platform, does not consider it binding on him, and, my word for it, he will be shorter by a head within three days after the annunciation. Sir, it is the Democratic platform; it is the party test. Any man who does not swear allegiance to the Dred Scott decision is no Democrat. I hold in my hand an exposition of that decision, from a Democratic newspaper published in the city of Washington, which I believe is universally admitted to be good Democratic authority. It is more than that; the newspaper to which I allude distills the pure essence, the very essential oil of Democracy. I allude to the Union newspaper of this city, some of whose articles are understood to be written by the President of the United States and to be supervised by his Cabinet, and to send forth the perfectly pure Democratic doctrine. I believe that when this pure

Democratic doctrine is seen, it will be offensive not only to the people of the North, but of the South likewise. But, sir, to the article. In the Union of November 17, 1857, appeared a long article, prepared with great care, evidently intended as a lasting exposition of the position of the Democratic party. It says:

"Slaves were recognized as property in the British colonies of North America, by the Government of Great Britain, by the colonial laws, and by the Constitution of the United States. Under these sanctions, vested rights have accrued to the amount of some $1,600,000,000. It is, therefore, the duty of Congress and the State Legislatures to protect that property.

"The Constitution declares that 'the citizens of each State shall be entitled to all the privileges and immunities of citizens in the several States.' Every citizen of one State coming into another State, has, therefore, a right to the protection of his person, and that property which is recognized as such by the Constitution of the United States; any law of a State to the contrary, notwithstanding. So far from any State having a right to deprive him of this property, it is its bounden duty to protect him in its possession.

"If these views are correct, (and we believe it would be difficult to invalidate them,) it follows that all State laws, whether organic or otherwise, which prohibit a citizen of one State from settling in another, and bringing his slave property with him, and most especially declaring it forfeited, are direct violations of the original intention of a government which, as before stated, is the protection of person and property, and of the Constitution of the United States, which recognizes property in slaves, and declares that 'the citizens of each State shall be entitled to all the privileges and immunities of citizens in the several States,' among the most essential of which is the protection of persons and property.

"What is recognized as property by the Constitution of the United States, by a provision which applies equally to all the States, has an inalienable right to be protected in all the States."

There you see the doctrine announced, that the States are under obligation to protect slave property, although it may be brought within their limits with the intention of keeping it there. The free States are compelled to protect slave property within their limits, although it may be brought there for the purpose of remaining, under the doctrine here laid down; and if the Dred Scott decision be law, or if it be hereafter regarded as a law, this reasoning is correct. If the Constitution of the United States carries slave property one inch beyond the jurisdiction of the State law creating or regulating it, it carries it everywhere; for no person can "be deprived of life, liberty, or property, without due process of law;" but we deny, *in toto*, that the Constitution of the United States does recognize or regulate or acknowledge property in slaves.

In this connection, let me allude to a remark of the Senator from Georgia, [Mr. IVERSON.] Some days ago he told us what he would deem a sufficient cause for a dissolution of this Union. That I may not misrepresent him, I will read exactly what he said. He declared:

"Sir, it is not so difficult a matter to dissolve this Union as many believe. Let the Republican party of the North obtain possession of the Government, and pass a Wilmot proviso; or abolish slavery in the District of Columbia; or repeal the fugitive slave law; or reform the Supreme Court, and annul the Dred Scott decision; or do any other act infringing upon the rights, impairing the equality, or wounding the honor of the slave States; or let them elect a President upon the avowed declaration and principle that freedom and slavery cannot exist together in the Union, and that one or the other must give way, and be sacrificed to the other, and the Union would be dissolved in six months."

Now, sir, I propose to do two or three things, which the honorable Senator from Georgia declares are good and sufficient reasons for dissolving this Union. I do not speak for the Republican party; I speak for myself. I say I do propose the reorganization of the Supreme Court. The present organization of that court is monstrous. Judge McLean has as many causes to try in his circuit as have all the five slaveholding judges put together. When he was appointed justice of that circuit, it was a howling wilderness; now there are a thousand millions of commerce within it. Then he could hold a court in every State in his circuit; now he cannot reach some of those States once in five years. I propose to reorganize that court, so as to make it conform to the business of the country. I propose that its judges shall be located so that they can at least visit every State in the district once or twice a year; and in order to do that, the court must be reorganized. Three fourths of the entire business of the courts of the United States is at the North, where you have four judges of the Supreme Court. One fourth of it is at the South, where you have five. I propose to reorganize that court; and, if the Senator from Georgia were in his seat, I would ask him how he proposes to dissolve the Union after it is done? I ask any Senator, who is blustering in the Senate or elsewhere about dissolving this Union, how he is going to do it?

We propose to do more; we mean to elect a President who entertains the same views; and if that be a just cause for dissolving this Union, again I ask, how are you going to do it? I want any man on this floor to tell me how he is going to dissolve this Union, because we, the people of the United States, see fit to exercise our constitutional privilege. We mean to annul the Dred Scott decision—no, sir, I take that back; it is no decision. We do not think it is a decision at all. The only point decided in that case was, that negroes cannot come into court. That we accept; that we cannot annul; that is decided; but the stump speeches of Chief Justice Taney, and the other judges, were mere fanfaronade, meaning nothing. It was not a decision of the court; and if we elect our President in 1860, *as we are going to do*, that decision will never be made. I do not say that that decision would not now be made. I think if a case were before the court now, it would make the Dred Scott decision legal; but the Supreme Court has always sided with the Administration in power. What did General Jackson do when the Supreme Court declared the United States Bank constitutional? Did he bow in deference to the opinions of the Supreme Court? No, sir; he scorned the opinion of the Supreme Court, and said that he would construe the Constitution for himself; that he was sworn to do it. I, sir, shall do the same thing. I have sworn to support the Constitution of the United States, and I have sworn to support it as the fathers made it, and not as the Supreme Court has altered it, and I never will swear allegiance to that. But I am not quite through with the Union article. It says further:

"The protection of property being next to that of person, the most important object of all good government, and property in slaves being recognized by the Constitution of the United States, as well as originally by all the old thirteen States, we have never doubted that the emancipation of slaves in those States where it previously existed, by an arbitrary act of the Legislature, was a gross violation of the rights of property."

There you have it declared that abolition of

slavery in seven of the old thirteen States was unconstitutional, and, according to the Dred Scott decision, it was. I ask any man of common sense—I will not ask a lawyer; I am no lawyer myself—but I ask any man of common sense, if he believes that the old thirteen States, seven of which intended to abolish slavery within a very few years, would have adopted a Constitution which prohibited them from doing the very act which they contemplated doing *instanter?* I ask any man if he believes for a single moment that the Representatives of those seven States that intended immediately to abolish slavery within their borders, would ever have assented to a Constitution which prohibited them from doing the very act which they proposed to do? No, sir, the proposition is absurd; and the judges of the Supreme Court themselves did not believe it when they uttered it. No man of common sense can believe it. It is not so.

But, sir, monstrous as is this proposition, monstrous as is the article which I have read, if the Dred Scott decision be law it is all true; and it is a mere question of time when every State of this Union will become a slave State. If the honorable Senator from Louisiana, or any other man, should see fit to take a thousand negroes into the State of Michigan after that decision shall have become the law, I defy any power short of a revolution in this Government to prevent him, or take them from him. But, sir, it is not law; it is not common sense; yet this Dred Scott decision is the only platform of the Democratic party at the present time—the only issue before the country. I beg pardon; there is another issue, not yet perfected, and that is this $30,000,000 bribery and corruption fund. That is to be another plank in the Democratic platform. These two planks, the Dred Scott decision and Cuba, are to be the platform that is to float the party into power if it ever arrives there; the Dred Scott decision and the $30,000,000 loan, with, perhaps, the honorable Senator from Virginia [Mr. HUNTER] astride of them; and with that platform and that candidate, the Democratic party will march to certain defeat.

But, sir, as this measure at the present time is a financial question, I propose very briefly to allude to the financial condition of the country. I look upon this as the practical method of judging of its merits. I hold in my hand a letter written by a very distinguished man, at present connected with this Government, dated March 1, 1852, and addressed to a committee of gentlemen of Baltimore. It is signed "James Buchanan." It says:

> "We must inscribe upon our banners, a sound regard for the reserved rights of the States, a strict construction of the Constitution, a denial to Congress of all powers not clearly granted by that instrument, and a rigid economy in public expenditures.
>
> "These expenditures have now reached the enormous sum of $50,000,000 per annum, and unless arrested in their advance by the strong arm of the Democracy of the country, may, in the course of a few years, reach $100,000,000."

Well, sir, "the strong arm of the Democracy" has been managing our affairs ever since. The President of the United States was then mistaken a few millions as to the expenditures; for the entire expenditures of 1852, including payment of the public debt, was only $44,481,447; but let him have the advantage of his own figures. The strong arm of the Democracy has had charge of this Government from that time to the present, and we have already reached the point that he prophesied we might reach in a few years—$100,000,000 of expenditure. It was demonstrated to my entire satisfaction, and, I believe, to the satisfaction of the Senate, by the honorable Senator from Kentucky, [Mr. CRITTENDEN,] the other day, that $100,000,000 would not pay the expenses of Government for this year. I propose a change; I propose that we try some other hand at economizing the expenses of this Government. But let me go on with the letter. Its writer says further:

> "The appropriation of money to accomplish great national objects, sanctioned by the Constitution, ought to be on a scale commensurate with our power and resources as a nation; but its expenditure ought to be conducted under the guidance of enlightened economy and strict responsibility. I am convinced that our expenses might be considerably reduced, below the present standard, not only without detriment, but with positive advantage both to the Government and the people."

If the expenditures could then be reduced below $50,000,000 with advantage to the Government and the people, what can be done now? Is there any reason why our expenditures should be greater now than they were in 1852? There is no reason except that money may be used for purposes of corruption; and I propose to examine into some of these corruptions now and here. This letter says further:

> "An excessive and lavish expenditure of public money, though in itself highly pernicious, is as nothing when compared with the disastrous influence it may exert upon the character of our free institutions. A strong tendency towards extravagance is the great political evil of the present day; and this ought to be firmly resisted."

Sir, I propose to resist it with all the firmness God has given me. Now, let us look a little into the expenditures of this Government. I hold in my hand an official document of the Senate, printed at the last session, giving the receipts and expenditures of the Government from its formation to 1857; and I desire to present some facts which are shown by this document; and to be as brief as possible, I will take it by decades, and I will commence with the military service of the country. In 1790, the whole expenses of the Army amounted, in round numbers, to $917,000; in 1800, $3,272,000; in 1810, $3,107,920; in 1820, $4,923,027; in 1830, $5,082,843; in 1840, $6,504,830; in 1850, $6,838,919; and in 1857, $18,614,594. This last sum does not include all the expenditures of the Army for 1857; for Senators will recollect that one of the first bills we passed at the last session was a bill making an appropriation of $5,700,000 for deficiencies in the expenses of the Army. Thus it will be seen that the Army expenses alone, from 1850 to 1857, almost quadrupled, and this in a time of profound peace. Does any Senator on this floor believe there was any necessity for such an enormous increase in the expenditures for the Army? Does any man believe that a prudent administration of the Government would not cut down the Army expenditures at least one half? Sir, the extravagance is enormous and outrageous; and it requires something more than the strong hand of the Democratic party to rectify the evil. We will take it in the strong hand of Republicanism, and then we will remedy it.

But, sir, let us look at the Navy. In 1800, the expenditures for the Navy were $3,042,352;

in 1810, $1,870,274; in 1820, $2,709,243; in 1830, $3,496,643; in 1840, $7,562,752; in 1850, $9,571,646; in 1857, $14,117,434. Have we any more ships, or any more guns, or any more efficient force, to-day, than we had in 1850? I am informed that we have not. On the contrary, it is said, I know not with how much truth, that our Navy is hardly as efficient as it was at that time. At any rate, we have had no war, no extraordinary demand for excessive naval expenditures, and yet they have been reaching up until they are $14,000,000.

There is one other account here, to which I wish to call the attention of the Senate. It is headed "miscellaneous expenditures." I do not know exactly what constitute the miscellaneous expenditures of this Government, but I notice a most extraordinary increase in them of late. I take it for granted that what cannot be charged anywhere to anything, goes down as miscellaneous. The miscellaneous expenditures of this Government in 1800 amounted to $312,823; in 1810, $650,514; in 1820, $1,386,448; in 1830, $1,436,201; in 1840, $3,243,649; in 1849, $3,595,853; and in 1857, $20,442,860. I should like to know how these miscellaneous expenditures have swollen so enormously. There is another remarkable fact connected with the great increase of the miscellaneous expenditures of the Government. I notice that when any very great outrage is about to be perpetrated, the miscellaneous expenditures increase enormously. In 1849 they were $3,595,853; and they swelled in 1850, when the fugitive slave bill was passed, to $7,122,970. Again, when the Missouri compromise was repealed, I notice they reached the enormous amount of $19,899,000; and a goodly portion of this great increase may be legitimately charged to the negroes. That institution has been a very expensive one to this Government. It has cost, in my estimation, all it is worth. When any great outrage was to be perpetrated, the expenditures of all branches of this Government have swollen enormously. So when the Lecompton constitution came here to be passed last winter. We have not got the account yet, but you will find an enormous expenditure in several of the Departments of this Government, which, the less said about, the better the parties interested will be satisfied.

As I said the other day, we have had a bill under consideration in the Committee on Commerce to reduce the expenditures for the collection of the revenue over $600,000 a year, and we have not commenced the work of reform even at that. We have lopped off by that bill a thousand useless employēs of the Government, scattered over the United States; but we have not probed the wound to the bottom. As I have said, that bill, if it becomes a law, will save $600,000 a year. I propose, for a moment, to call attention to some of the outrageous expenditures connected with that Department. In the Passamaquoddy district, at Eastport, Maine, the whole amount of revenue collected for the year ending June 30, 1857, was $14,285 33, and the expense of collecting it was $22,357 71; and nineteen men were employed to collect $14,000 of revenue. In Frenchman's bay district, at Ellsworth, they collected $954 96, and the expenses were $5,032 09; and it took ten men to collect the $954. At Wiscassett, in Maine, you collected $130 93; and it cost $7,359 09, and took eight men to collect $130. These are samples. At Portsmouth, New Hampshire, the revenue collected was $5,530 54; the expense of collection was $10,984 49, and twenty-one men were employed to make the collection. At Burlington, Vermont, the revenue was $8,581 70; the expense of collecting was $16,285 47, and thirty-three men were employed to collect it. At Marblehead, Massachusetts, the revenue was $250 85; the expense of collecting it $2,228 97, and nine men were employed to collect it. At Plymouth, in Massachusetts, the revenue collected was $395 12; the expense of collection was $3,216 04, and six men were employed to make the collection. At Barnstable, Massachusetts, the revenue collected, was $1,462 75: the expense of collection $11,953 20, and nineteen men were employed to make the collection. At Nantucket, Massachusetts, the revenue collected was $95 81; the expense of collecting it was $2,320 73, and three men were employed in the collection. At New London, in Connecticut, the revenue collected was $3,223 89; the cost of collecting it was $29,789 48, and seven men were employed in its collection. At Oswego, in New York, the revenue collected was $6,149 09; the cost of collecting it $18,214 58, and twenty-three men were employed in its collection. At Niagara, New York, the revenue collected was $8,284 85; the cost of collecting it $12,296 92, and nineteen men were employed in its collection. At Buffalo, New York, the revenue collected was $10,140 53; the cost of collecting it was $16,896 51, and twenty men were employed in its collection. At Cape Vincent, New York, the revenue collected was $2,098 12; the cost of collecting it $7,138 87, and thirteen men were employed in its collection. I might continue the citations; but these will suffice.

True, we shall have lopped off these things by that bill, if it shall become a law; but I hold that these extravagant expenditures of the Government ought never to have been commenced; and I hold this Administration responsible for the enormous abuses that have crept into the collection of the revenue. The head of the Department had no right, under the law, to appoint inspectors; but he could appoint clerks and porters and boatmen, and a thousand other officers, and pay them the highest salary at his discretion; and under the abuse of that power these enormous expenditures have sprung up. You may go into any of the Departments of this Government, and you will find the same kind of abuse existing. Go into any bureau in this city, and you will find abuses. It requires an honest Administration of this Government; it requires a man who dares to take the responsibility of doing right; and then you may reduce your expenditures, as Mr. Buchanan suggested in the letter I have quoted, in my opinion, below $50,000,000; but we have tried the Democratic party; we have weighed them in the balance, and found them wanting. We do not propose to try them again. We propose to thrust out the corrupt, the lavish men, who now control the Government, and put in honest men, who will retrench in good earnest; not men who will write letters recommending retrenchment, but men who will take hold and do the work of retrenchment.

I have placed the expenditures of the Government this year at $95,000,000. I know not how much will be appropriated, but I know that if the

Government pays its debts this year, and does not leave a deficiency for the next Congress to provide for, the expenses will be $100,000,000; but I take the basis of expenditure to be $95,000,000. Taking it at $95,000,000, without counting the sum of $30,000,000 for Cuba, in this bill, or the $200,000,000 for the purchase of Cuba, but simply taking the regular expenses, the cost of running the institution, and the quota of each congressional district would be $405,982; and the State of Michigan, upon the present basis of representation, would have to pay $1,623,928, but in truth the proportion of the State of Michigan is over three millions of this enormous expenditure for the support of this Government. The State of Maine pays $2,435,892, upon the present basis; the State of New Hampshire $1,217,846; the State of Vermont, $1,217,846; the State of Massachusetts, $4,465,802; the State of Rhode Island, $811,964; the State of Ohio, $8,525,622; the State of Indiana, $4,465,802; the State of Illinois, $3,653,838; the State of Iowa, $811,964; and so on. If this revenue was collected by direct taxation—and I wish it were tried for once—my word for it, the expenditures of this Government would be reduced more than one half before the expiration of twelve months from this day. It is because the people do not see how, and where, and when they are taxed, that the expenses of the Federal Government have increased so enormously. It would create a rebellion in ninety days from this time, if you were to send your tax-collectors around to the different congressional districts, to wrench from the pockets of the tax-payers $405,000. They would not stand it for a day; but because you can cover up these extravagances, because you can borrow money and leave future generations to pay it, these things are permitted; the expenditures go on, and God only knows where they will end. As I said before, we have tried the Democratic party; we have weighed it in the balance; we have found it wanting; and we propose, in 1860, to take possession of this Government, and not have Cuba, either.

Printed at the Congressional Globe Office.

KANSAS--THE LECOMPTON CONSTITUTION.

SPEECH

OF

HON. Z. CHANDLER, OF MICHIGAN.

Delivered in the Senate of the United States, March 12, 1858.

Mr. CHANDLER. Mr. President, it was not my intention originally to participate in the debate on the Lecompton constitution. I had intended to leave the subject to older and abler and more experienced colleagues; but the occasion seems to me to be so great, and the consequences which may result from our decision so dangerous, that I cannot permit this bill to pass without, at least, entering my protest against it. I shall oppose this bill for the following reasons: First, because the whole matter was conceived and executed in fraud; second, because this constitution does not emanate from the people of Kansas Territory, or express their will; third, because it is one of a series of aggressions on the part of the slave power, which, if permitted to be consummated, must end in the subversion of the Constitution and the Union; and, fourth, because it strikes a death blow at State sovereignty and popular rights. I shall proceed as briefly as possible to give the reasons upon which I base these objections.

It is well known, sir, that, at the close of the revolutionary war, and at the formation of this Federal Government, all the States of the Union were slave States, but all looked upon slavery as an unmitigated evil; and all looked forward hopefully to the day when it should no longer exist. No man, then, was bold enough to advocate the extension of slavery or even its long continuance, but all looked forward to an early period when it should cease to exist. These views being prevalent throughout the land, one of the early acts of the Continental Congress was the adoption of the ordinance of 1787, forever prohibiting slavery and involuntary servitude in all the then Territories of these United States. This was itself a southern measure to a considerable extent, although, at that time, there was no diversity of opinion in regard to it. Some of the northern States, as was well known, intended to abolish slavery at a very early day, while some of the southern States desired that it might be deferred to a much later period. Those States which expected to be cursed, as they then termed it, with the institution for a longer period, desired the power of reclaiming their fugitives from service or labor if they should escape. Those States that proposed soon to abolish the institution yielded that power; and upon that compromise the ordinance of 1787 was adopted. Many of the members of the Constitutional Convention were likewise members of the Continental Congress, and the ordinance of 1787 was one of the compromises which led to the adoption of the Constitution itself; and, without that ordinance, it is extremely doubtful whether that instrument would ever have been adopted by the States.

This was a finality upon the slavery question. It settled that question forever. No further agitation ever could take place upon the subject of slavery, it was supposed, under that compromise. The settlement was this: slavery was a creature of municipal law; it was left to the States in which it then existed to continue it or abolish it, whenever they might see fit; and in all the Territories of the United States it was forever prohibited. This was the finality of a finality. There never could be any further agitation of the question of slavery in the Union, under it.

Under this settlement, the country remained in peace for more than thirty years. No agitation of the subject took place, and none could take place, for it was not in a position to be agitated. I say the country remained in peace for more than thirty years, and until the State of Missouri applied for admission into the Union as a slave State. During the intermediate time, the Louisiana territory had been purchased, and Louisiana had been admitted as a slave State, without objection on the part of the North. It was quietly assented to; scarcely a protest was entered against it; but when Missouri applied for admission as a slave State, the North objected to the admission of any more slave States, and declared that it was not only distinctly understood, but agreed to, that no more slave States should ever be admitted into this Union. The North claimed that that was the basis of the original compromise—the ordinance of 1787. Agitation ran high. The South then, as now, threatened a dissolution of the Union, unless all her imperious demands were assented to. The North then, as now, denied her right or her power to dissolve the Union for any such reason, or for any reason.

During this excitement the hearts of brave men quailed in view of the danger to the Constitution and the Union, and finally a proposition of compromise was brought into Congress from the South, as a southern measure. The compromise was upon this basis: you of the North consent to the admission of Missouri as a slave State, with the tacit understanding that when Arkansas applies she shall likewise be admitted as a slave State; and we will guaranty to you forever that the ordinance of 1787 shall be spread over all the territory lying north of thirty sixth degrees and thirty minutes. So utterly objectionable was this compromise to the North, that not a single man who voted for it was ever heard of again, politically, at the North. Each northern man who voted for that compromise voted for his own death-warrant, politically—not as has been asserted at the North, because they voted to prohibit slavery north of thirty-six degrees thirty minutes, but because they voted to admit the State of Missouri as a slave State into this Union. For that they were blamed, and not for assenting to the restrictive line.

But, sir, the compromise was adopted, and peace again reigned throughout the land. The question was settled, and settled forever. Here was another finality, so far as agitation upon that subject was concerned. The South was to have the State of Missouri and the State of Arkansas by tacit consent, whenever she should apply for admission into the Union; the North, as an equivalent, was guarantied all of that territory lying north of thirty-six degrees thirty minutes, forever. The South received her equivalent in the States of Missouri and Arkansas; the North waited patiently for the day when she should receive hers. The compromise was acquiesced in, and again the country had peace, so far as agitation on the slavery question was concerned, and continued at peace, with some slight ripples here and there, until Texas applied for admission into the Union. Then again there was an agitation; then again the Union was threatened, and threatened from the South; then again another compromise was entered into; to wit, a renewal of the Missouri line. The country remained in peace until, in process of time, a new light broke upon the vision of the people of these United States; to wit, the light of popular sovereignty. It so happened that many of the slave States, during the fall of 1847, in solemn political conventions resolved that they would support no man for the Presidency who was not opposed to the principles of the Wilmot Proviso, so called. In December, 1847, my illustrious predecessor, for reasons best known to himself—although he had time and again expressed his regret that the Hon. John Davis, of Massachusetts, should have talked against time to the end of a session, thus depriving him of the power of recording his vote for the Wilmot Proviso—wrote the "Nicholson letter," in which he said:

"But certain it is that the principle of interference should not be carried beyond the necessary implication which produces it. It should be 'limited to the creation of proper governments for 'new countries, acquired or settled, and to the necessary provision for their eventual admission into 'the Union, leaving, in the mean time, to the people 'inhabiting them to regulate their internal concerns 'in their own way. They are just as capable of 'doing so as the people of the States."

Here, sir, permit me to say, you find the basis of the Democratic Cincinnati platform, which has been commented on time and again; here you find the basis of the Kansas-Nebraska bill; and, in fact, you find the basis of this very Lecompton constitution in the Nicholson letter. This was the first time this doctrine was inaugurated at the North: scarcely a man at the South ever uttered the sentiment. But I will read further:

"Briefly, then, I am opposed to the exercise of 'any jurisdiction by Congress over this matter; 'and I am in favor of leaving to the people of any 'territory which may be hereafter acquired the 'right to regulate it for themselves, under the 'general principles of the Constitution."

"Subject only to the Constitution," I believe, in the new version; but this is the original text.

"Leave to the people who will be affected by 'this question, to adjust it upon their own responsibility, and in their own manner, and we shall 'render another tribute to the principles of our 'Government, and furnish another guarantee for 'its permanence and prosperity."

There, sir, is the original of this great fraud upon the North, yclept "popular sovereignty," and "perfect freedom for the people of a Territory to regulate their domestic institutions in their own way." It is true, that when the doctrine of squatter sovereignty was first introduced, some of the gentlemen on the other side of the Chamber entered a faint protest, but it was so faint that it never reached the ears of northern men; and when on the stump, before the people of my State, I asserted that the doctrine which is now introduced here as the doctrine of the Constitution, was the doctrine of the Democratic party, I was told that that was not the doctrine of the Democratic party; that it was merely the opinion of some few southern fire-eaters; that the great national Democratic party was firmly planted on the principles of squatter sovereignty, the right of the people of the Territories to regulate their domestic institutions in their own way, including the institution of slavery.

Sir, up to the writing of the Nicholson letter, the right of Congress to make all needful rules and regulations for the Territories of the United States was never called in question. No Executive of the United States ever doubted it; no Congress of the United States ever doubted their full power to legislate for the Territories as they saw fit; and up to that date the Supreme Court never doubted the power of Congress to legislate on slavery in the Territories. That was the inauguration of a new principle; to wit, the principle of squatter sovereignty—not popular sovereignty, as is here explained, but squatter sovereignty—the right of the people to introduce or prohibit slavery in the Territories, while they were in a territorial condition.

The South held up the glittering fantasy of a presidential nomination before the eager eyes of the northern aspirants for that honor, and at the same time exhibited the Nicholson letter, as the highest bid yet made, and asked, "Who bids higher?" Mr. Fillmore followed with the fugitive slave law and the compromise measures of 1850. Mr. Webster followed again, with his 7th of March speech; and last, though not least, came the repeal of the Missouri compromise line.

I do not propose to discuss the repeal of the Missouri compromise. If I should enter upon that discussion, I should only weary the Senate, for I should not know where to leave off. I look upon it as the greatest fraud ever perpetrated before the eyes of this nation. The price had been paid, and the terms of the bargain were repudiated after one side had received the equivalent. It was a violation of a solemn compact. But I do not propose to go into the discussion of it at this time.

But, sir, how did you pay those men who were bidding and overbidding, and outbidding each other for presidential nominations? First, to the writer of the Nicholson letter you gave the empty honor of a nomination for the Presidency, and then defeated him by southern votes; to the second, you refused even the poor compliment of a nomination in a national convention, when it was well known to everybody that under no circumstances could he have been elected if he had received the nomination. The third you consigned to the grave. He received but four southern votes in the convention to which I have just referred, and it broke his heart. The fourth you are now pursuing with all the powers of this Government; with the keen scent of the blood-hound; you are after his scalp; and yet, sir, this Administration owes to him, more than to any other man, its present possession of power. There are three men in this nation to whom the present Administration owe their present position more than to any other three thousand men in the United States. Those men it is needless for me to name, although I will do so. One of them is the Senator from Illinois, [Mr. DOUGLAS,] another Mr. Walker, late Governor of Kansas, and the third is John W. Forney, of Pennsylvania. But for these men, James Buchanan, President of the United States, would be rusticating at Wheatland, instead of occupying the White House. Poor pay indeed have they got for their subserviency to southern interests, and their rejection of the principles upon which they had previously acted.

Mr. President, while all these aggressions of the slave power were made their cry was, "stand by the Constitution and the Union." I have heard it from every stump in Michigan: it was the rallying cry while they were undermining the Constitution and sapping the foundation of this Union. Although I am not a lawyer, I wish to refer to two or three clauses of the Constitution of the United States; for I claim that it is so plain in language and its intent so transparent, "that the wayfaring man, though a fool, need not err therein." I do not believe that it requires any hair-splitting of lawyers to comprehend that immortal instrument, the Constitution of the United States. It is true that the Supreme Court has endeavored to mystify two or three of its plainest provisions in its late opinion, or late speeches, delivered on a question that was not before it; but, sir, it does not require a lawyer, in my estimation, to show that the instrument is not what they are attempting to make it, and what the framers of it abhorred, a pro-slavery instrument. I claim that slaves are not recognized as property in that instrument anywhere. They lay great stress upon that clause of the Constitution which protects the slave trade for twenty years. I consider that fully, fairly, and forever answered by the honorable Senator from Maine, [Mr. FESSENDEN.] If property in slaves, he said, is based upon that clause of the Constitution allowing the slave trade for twenty years, of course, at the end of those twenty years, that property ceases to receive the protection of that clause of the Constitution; it extends protection to it only for twenty years. But I shall say no more upon that point. There is, however, one other clause upon which the court dwells yet more fully, and that is the fugitive-slave clause, so called.

"No person held to service or labor in one State, 'under the laws thereof, escaping into another, 'shall, in consequence of any law or regulation 'therein, be discharged from such service or labor, 'but shall be delivered up, on claim of the party 'to whom such service or labor may be due."

Not giving a lawyer's opinion, but the opinion of a man of common sense, if you please, I should say that if that clause proved anything at all, it proved the direct reverse of what the Supreme Court endeavored to make it prove. Is it necessary to introduce into the Constitution a clause protecting property already protected by the very instrument into which that clause is introduced? If slaves were property under the Constitution, were they not property everywhere? If they were protected as property, were they not so protected everywhere? The proposition is an absurdity; and, if there were no other clause in the Constitution upon that point, I should say that that proved conclusively that they were not recognized as property under the general clauses of the Constitution. What would have been thought of a clause like this: "that horses, sheep, cattle, mules, &c., escaping from one State into another, shall be given up on proof of ownership to the person to whom such property belongs?" and yet such a clause would be just as appropriate as that on the subject of fugitive slaves, if they were recognized as property under the Constitution. There was no such right claimed as property in man at that day; and, as was remarked by the honorable Senator from New Hampshire [Mr. HALE] the other day, even the word "servitude," which was in the first draft of that clause of the Constitution, was stricken out on the motion of a distinguished Virginia gentleman, and the word "service" introduced, because servitude might be construed to mean slaves, and service could not. The whole of the debates upon the adoption of the Constitution, show that its framers never meant that it should recognize slaves as property. If they had intended it, is it not a little singular that nowhere throughout the entire instrument can the word "slave" be found, or anything that can be tortured, or ever has been tortured, heretofore, into a recognition of slaves as property, under the Constitution?

But again, sir, so far from recognizing slaves as property, they spread the common law over that

Constitution; they adopted the common law as part and parcel of the Constitution; and it is well known, and settled in numerous cases, that the common law does not, and never has claimed to, recognize property in slaves. Here is a decision of the Supreme Court of Georgia, in 1851:

"I now consider the decision of the English 'courts, upon the subject of slavery, and I think 'it will be seen that slavery has never been recog-'nized to exist there under the common law. On 'the contrary, it is well settled that the moment a 'slave, whether African, Indian, Jew, or Gentile, 'sets his foot upon British soil he is a freeman, and 'entitled to the protection of the laws as such."—*Neal* vs. *Farmer*, 9 *Georgia Reports*, p. 568.

Lord Mansfield, in his opinion in the Sommersett case, declared:

"So high an act of dominion must be recognized 'by the law of the country where it is used. The 'power of a master over his slave has been ex-'tremely different in different countries. The 'state of slavery is of such a nature that it is in-'capable of being introduced on any reasons, 'moral or political, but only by positive law, which 'preserves its force long after the reasons, occa-'sion, and time itself from whence it was created, 'are erased from memory."—*Howell's State Trials*, vol. 20, p. 82.

Innumerable cases might be cited to prove that the common law does not, and never did, recognize property in slaves; and yet the framers of the Constitution spread that law all over the Constitution, instead of saying that slaves were property.

What was the object of the Supreme Court, in traveling out of the record to show that the Constitution did, or would, if the case were brought before them, recognize property in slaves? I look upon this as one of the most dangerous aggressions which has ever been attempted upon the Constitution of the United States. Their object was covered up; it was not announced; you may hear it in private conversation, but it has never been announced publicly. The object was insidiously, first, to recognize slaves under the Constitution; secondly, to make out, by construction of the property clause, that the Constitution itself carried slaves everywhere. They declared in that decision that the Constitution carried slaves into a Territory. Well, sir, if the Constitution carries slaves anywhere outside of the limits of the municipal law creating slavery, it carries them everywhere. If slaves are property under the Constitution, Michigan is as much a slave State to-day as South Carolina, if any man or set of men see fit to take slaves there. They are protected under this property clause, if they are property under the Constitution; but we deny that they are. We deny the authority of the Supreme Court to insert any new provision into the Constitution making them property. Here is the clause which it is said carries slavery now into any Territory, if it is carried there; and the same clause will carry it into any State, by the same rule. They dare not attempt, at this time, to break down State sovereignty; they dare not assert their whole meaning; but they take it piece-meal. The clause in which they pretend to find this power is that which declares that no citizen shall "be deprived of life, liberty, or property, without due process of law; nor shall private property be taken for public use without just compensation."

That is the clause which they mean to render effective; under which they are endeavoring to strengthen slavery by their illegal decision, as I regard it.

That is not the last aggression. After having established the property clause, and carried slavery all over these United States, there is something left to be done. The intention is then—it has ceased to be problematical—to open the African slave trade. Why not give us the whole dose at once—property clause, African slave trade, and all? Why, sir, you southern men are more cruel than the heathen gods. They were satisfied with the sacrifice of hecatombs of human victims; but you take one hecatomb after another. You sacrificed one in adopting the Missouri compromise line; another in repealing it; and now you sacrifice another in passing the Lecompton constitution; anon you will sacrifice another in spreading this property clause; and afterwards you will sacrifice another hecatomb in opening the African slave trade. Why not take all your victims at once, swallow them *en masse*, and let future generations live? You do not appreciate your northern tools; you are afraid to crowd them too far; you are afraid to give them the whole dose at once; but I tell you, sir, that you cannot give them a dose that they will not swallow. You need not give it to them in homeopathic portions. Give them the slave trade, the property clause, and the whole series at once; for so long as your Federal patronage holds out, so long you can rely on your northern allies. You see they will swallow Lecompton —it does not require an effort—with all its frauds. They would take the property clause, and resolve to-morrow that every State in the Union is a slave State, and it would not require an effort for them to get down that doctrine. Then you might introduce the African slave trade, and they would take that with the same facility that they take all the rest. Do not fear to crowd them, sir. They are few, and growing beautifully less, rapidly, but they are reliable just as long as you have the Government with its patronage.

I come now, sir, to the first organization of the Territory of Kansas under the bill of 1854. The first election under that act was for a Delegate to Congress. At that election there was no very great violence attempted, but there was fraud. Some nineteen hundred Missourians, I think, actually passed over into the Territory, voted in General Whitfield, and then went home. That terminated that campaign; but between the election of General Whitfield and the election of the members of the Legislative Council, there was a large influx of population from the North. It was deemed important then to strike a final blow for the institution of slavery in Kansas; then the forces were organized and drilled; they were organized in companies and regiments, with muskets and cannon, with bowie knives and revolvers, with baggage wagons, tents, and whiskey. Under banners inscribed "for Kansas and slavery," they marched over and took possession of the land. They went to every voting precinct in the whole Territory of Kansas except one, and they drove from the polls the honest settlers of that Territory, and from their seats the judges of election appointed by the Governor of the Territory. By a comparison of the census returns with the poll-books of the Territory, and by the oral testimony of more than three hundred witnesses under oath, it is proven that four thousand nine hundred votes were cast in that Territory for members of the Legislature, by persons who were not residents of Kansas.

Very much has been said about a great influx of voters under the auspices of the Emigrant Aid Society. I have taken a little pains to ascertain just how many of the men sent out by the Emigrant Aid Society voted at that election. Four thousand nine hundred border ruffians from Missouri voted, and they left the Territory the next day; but of all the men who were ever sent to that Territory under the auspices of the Emigrant Aid Society, only thirty-seven voted on the 30th of March, 1855. Thirty-seven of the honest citizens sent out under the auspices of that society, who were there residents, cultivating the soil, cast their votes on that day, and no more. This is proved—proved beyond cavil or controversy: and it demonstrates that a great cry has been made over a small matter.

The members of the Legislature elected in this way applied to the Governor for certificates. Governor Reeder knew the frauds that had been perpetrated. He knew that not a man of them was entitled to a certificate; but many of the voting precincts were distant; and where there was no contestant he issued his certificates to these fraudulently elected men, most of them being Missourians. Where there was a contestant he ordered new elections; and in every such instance free-State men were elected, in place of the pro-slavery men previously said to have been elected. But, on the assembling of the Legislature, the first act was to wipe out these after elections—these honest elections—to throw out of the Legislature every man honestly elected; to organize, and proceed to enact a code of laws. In a very brief period they enacted laws that fill eight hundred and twenty-two pages. They took the whole code of Missouri, and after they got through they were afraid there might be some mistake somewhere, and they added the following addendum:

"Whenever the word 'State' occurs in any act 'of the present Legislative Assembly, or any law 'of this Territory, in such construction as to indicate the locality of the operation of such act or 'laws, the same shall in every instance be taken 'and understood to mean 'Territory,' and shall 'apply to the Territory of Kansas."

Their whole code would have been arrant nonsense, if they had not put in that singular addendum; for the word "State" was copied into almost every enactment. They carried most of the statutes of Missouri over there; but they were not satisfied with enacting the Missouri code; some of the Missouri laws were not sufficiently stringent for the Territory of Kansas, and they enacted a little postscript to the extent of four or five pages of laws, which met their views.

Mr. POLK. I wish to ask the Senator if he really means to assert, without qualification, as I understand him to say just now, that the entire Missouri code was adopted by the Legislature of Kansas? I wish to say, if he does, that he is mistaken.

Mr. CHANDLER. I presume they had not time to put in all the resolves the Legislature of Missouri had enacted, and the amendments to their enactments. I do not mean to say that there might not have been some additions to those laws; but, in the main, these eight hundred and twenty-two pages were taken from the Missouri code, except four or five pages of infamous laws to which I shall have occasion to allude in a few moments.

Mr. POLK. Will the Senator allow me to ask him to specify any one law there that is copied exactly from the Missouri code?

Mr. CHANDLER. I have not the Missouri code before me, but if I had time I could point out a great number. I have examined them, and in the main they are identically the same. If it were not so, I want to know why they adopted this little addendum? If it were not so, what does this clause mean?

Mr. POLK. I will state that that takes for granted that all those who voted there were from Missouri.

Mr. CHANDLER. More than six sevenths of them were, as I can prove at the other end of the Capitol. I can prove to your satisfaction, or to that of any man on this floor, that more than six-sevenths of the votes cast at that election were from Missouri. I will prove it by over three hundred witnesses. I will prove it by three men who spent weeks in comparing the census list with the poll list. I have the evidence on hand to prove what I assert.

Mr. POLK. I shall be glad to have you prove it.

Mr. CHANDLER. I can prove it at any time. I could send to the other House now, and get three men, and put them under oath, and they will swear to the truth of every word I say. It would take some time to go over the testimony.

Mr. POLK. I should like to know their names.

Mr. CHANDLER. William A. Howard and John Sherman; the other I forget. I go by the record. I shall have occasion to allude to certain of those laws that were not taken from the code of Missouri, but which were considered an improvement upon the Missouri code; but I pass them by for the present.

Under this code of laws the territorial government was organized; and the Army of the United States was sent there to enforce them. Men were hunted down by sheriffs and by *posses* from other States, by border-ruffians everywhere, under the color of law. Sir, the State of Michigan has over one thousand of her people in Kansas to-day. Three of her citizens, and many other good men, have been murdered in cold-blood. Two of them, Barber and Brown, I know were as good men as can be found on the face of the earth. The other—Gay—was Mr. Pierce's land agent for the Territory. He was a Nebraska pro-slavery Democrat. He was met one day, with his son, on the road, and asked whether he was for free-State or pro-slavery. He had become a little free-Statish in his views, and not dreaming of danger, he said, "I am a free-State man," and he was shot down; and his son, in attempting to defend his father, received a bullet in his hip, and is now a cripple, in Michigan. I speak with some feeling, sir. I have a right to speak with feeling. My own constituents, my own people, have been brutally murdered, and I should be recreant to my trust if I did not speak with feeling on this subject. I know the men from Michigan who are in Kansas to be as good men as can be found within these United States, and when any man says that the emigrants from Michigan to the Territory of Kansas are picked up from the purlieus of cities, I tell him he knows nothing about the subject, and that it is not true. They are as good men as the State of Michigan produces; they are honest and brave; they know their rights, and knowing, dare defend them.

I come next to the election of members of the constitutional convention. The laws to which I have referred were still in force. In the mean time the Governor had been changed three times, and Governor Walker was then in office. We are not left to assertion with regard to the frauds in the election of the constitutional convention. I refer you to Executive Document No. 8, for the present session, page 128. There I find a letter from the Hon. Robert J. Walker, Governor of Kansas, to the Hon. Lewis Cass, Secretary of State, supplied to us by the Department of State, in which Governor Walker says:

"On reference to the territorial law, under 'which the convention was assembled, thirty four 'regularly organized counties were named as elec-'tion districts for delegates to the convention. In 'each and all of these counties it was required by 'law that a census should be taken and the voters 'registered; and when this was completed, the 'delegates to the convention should be apportioned 'accordingly. In nineteen of these counties there 'was no census, and therefore there could be no 'such apportionment there of delegates based upon 'such census. And in fifteen of these counties 'there was no registry of voters.

"These fifteen counties, including many of the 'oldest organized counties of the Territory, were 'entirely disfranchised, and did not give, and (by 'no fault of their own) could not give a solitary 'vote for delegates to the convention. This result 'was superinduced by the fact that the Territorial 'Legislature appointed all the sheriffs and probate 'judges in all these counties, to whom was assigned 'the duty, by law, of making this census and 'registry. These officers were political partisans, 'dissenting from the views and opinions of the 'people of these counties, as proved by the elec-'tion in October last. These officers, from want 'of funds, as they allege, neglected or refused to 'take any census or make any registry in these 'counties, and, therefore, they were entirely dis-'franchised, and could not, and did not, give a 'single vote at the election for delegates to the 'constitutional convention. And here I wish to 'call attention to the distinction, which will ap-'pear in my inaugural address, in reference to 'those counties where the voters were fairly regis-'tered and did not vote. In such counties where 'a full and free opportunity was given to register 'and vote, and they did not choose to exercise 'that privilege, the question is very different from 'those counties where there was no census or re-'gistry, and no vote was given or could be given, 'however anxious the people might be to partici-'pate in the election of delegates to the conven-'tion. Nor could it be said these counties acqui-'esced, for whenever they endeavored by a sub-'sequent census or registry of their own to supply 'this defect, occasioned by the previous neglect of 'the territorial officers, the delegates thus chosen 'were rejected by the convention.

"I repeat, that in nineteen counties out of 'thirty-four there was no census. In fifteen 'counties out of thirty-four there was no registry, 'and not a solitary vote was given, or could be 'given, for delegates to the convention, in any one 'of these counties. Surely, then, it cannot be said 'that such a convention, chosen by scarcely more 'than one-tenth of the present voters of Kansas, 'represented the people of that Territory, and 'could rightfully impose a constitution upon them 'without their consent. These nineteen counties, 'in which there was no census, constituted a *ma-'jority* of the counties of the Territory; and these 'fifteen counties, in which there was no registry, 'gave a much larger vote, at the October election, 'even with the six months' qualification, than the 'whole vote given to the delegates who signed the 'Lecompton constitution, on the 7th November 'last."

Here the fact is shown that for the constitutional convention the people of Kansas did not and could not vote. It is not true, as has been asserted, that even in other counties, where a registry was taken, it was fairly taken. I was informed by the Mayor of Leavenworth, one of the oldest citizens there, said to be a man of wealth, certainly a man of respectability, that his own name was not placed on the registry list, nor were one half the names of the free-State settlers in that city. In every county where a registry was taken, it was taken fraudulently; free State men were left off, and pro-slavery men, who were never known or heard of in the Territory, were placed on the list.

When more than half the counties in that Territory were disfranchised; when no fair registry was taken; when the very parties who had defrauded the people twice in previous elections, were to count the votes and make up the poll lists, it is not surprising that the free-State men of Kansas did not and would not vote at the election for delegates. They could not vote, as is asserted by Governor Walker. This, it must be remembered, is the evidence of the favorite Governor, of James Buchanan's own selection. This is no free-State Abolitionist. This is a man who went there honestly intending to make Kansas a slave State if he could; but like all other honest men who have been sent to Kansas, he was very soon converted from the opinion that the ruffianism was on the side of the free-State people, and law, order, and peace on the other side. Sir, I believe that if you or any other member of this body—I care not who it be—were sent to Kansas as Governor, and should remain there three months, you or he would stand where Governor Walker stands to day. There is not a member of this Senate that I would not trust there; and I aver that such would be the result. But I shall allude to that matter hereafter. I now proceed to the submission of the constitution.

Illegally elected as it was—elected by only two thousand votes, when, as is asserted by Governor Walker, there were more voters in the counties where no registry was taken than cast at this election—the convention met. I assert it to be the truth that but for the pledges given by Governor Walker and Secretary Stanton, that convention would never have assembled in the Territory of Kansas. You had not United States bayonets enough there to have kept it in session but for the pledges given by Governor Walker and Secretary Stanton, that the constitution should be fairly submitted to a full vote of the people. But, sir, I come to the submission. President Buchanan, through his Secretary of State, General Lewis Cass, gave the following instructions to Mr. Walker when he went to Kansas as Governor:

"It is 'the imperative and indispensable duty 'of the Government of the United States to secure 'to every resident inhabitant the free and independent expression of his opinion by his vote. This 'sacred right of each individual must be preserved; 'and, 'that being accomplished, nothing can be 'fairer than to leave the people of a Territory free 'from all foreign interference to decide their own 'destiny for themselves, subject only to the Constitution of the United States.'"

Again:

"When such a constitution shall be submitted 'to the people of the Territory, they must be protected in the exercise of their right of voting 'for or against that instrument; and the fair expression of the popular will must not be interrupted by fraud or violence."

These are the instructions under which Governor Walker acted. Mark the words: "When such a constitution shall be submitted"—not when a slavery clause, but when the "constitution shall be submitted" to the people of the Territory—"they must be protected in the exercise of their right of voting for or against that instrument."

But again, on page 111 of the same document to which I have alluded, you will find, in General Cass's letter to Mr. Stanton, the same language reiterated as late as November 30, 1857:

"When such a constitution shall be submitted 'to the people of the Territory, they must be 'protected in the exercise of their right of voting 'for or against that instrument, and the fair expression of the popular will must not be interrupted by fraud or violence."

Here is iteration after iteration that the constitution should be submitted to the people, and that no fraud or violence should interefere with its fair submission. Then we come to the assurances given by Governor Walker, which satisfied the free-State people that it would be submitted, and submitted to a fair vote. He says, in his letter of July 15:

"It was, however, universally admitted that, 'but for the position assumed in my inaugural address, and emphatically repeated at Topeka, the 'people of Kansas, so far as my power extended, 'should be permitted, by a full vote of the actual 'residents of Kansas, to decide upon the great 'question of the adoption or rejection of the State 'constitution to be prepared by the constitutional 'convention which should assemble at Lecompton 'in September next, that the more violent course 'would have prevailed, and the Territory have 'been immediately involved in a general and sanguinary civil war, postponing, for the present at 'least, if not indefinitely, any pacific settlement of 'these momentous questions."

He says further, in the same letter:

"I urged that they were pursuing a course in 'opposition to the laws, which never could lead to 'any successful result, and urged them to unite in 'voting for or against the adoption of such a constitution as might be submitted for their consideration by the constitutional convention which 'would assemble in September next, on the call of 'the Territorial Legislature. I endeavored to 'convince them that the so-called Republican party 'of Kansas, and their associates in the United 'States, had endeavored, and still desired, as set 'forth in their platform, to deprive the people of 'Kansas of the right to adopt their own social institutions, and had referred this question to Congress, where the people of the Territory would 'have no vote whatever; and continued my efforts 'on this ground, in connection with other topics, 'to separate the free-State Democrats from any 'alliance with the Republicans."

Here we get the meat in the cocoanut at last: "'to separate free-State Democrats from any alliance with Republicans." They were going to destroy the Republican party then! These pledges were given in the broadest and most emphatical manner—given everwhere—from the stump—from the rostrum—in private conversation, and everywhere throughout that Territory. Gov. Walker, under the instructions which I have read you from James Buchanan, through his Secretary of State, Lewis Cass, that it should be submitted, gave them the most positive assurances that, in any event, this constitution should be submitted to a fair vote of the people. Then, speaking of the Democratic convention in Kansas, he says:

"A resolution was offered by a pro-slavery delegate, instructing the nominee of the party for 'Congress to support there the adoption of the 'State constitution, which might be framed by the 'constitutional convention which should assemble 'in September next, whether the same had been 'submitted for ratification by the vote of the 'people or not. Very able addresses were made 'on this resolution, and especially by Judge Elmore, of Alabama, who earnestly advocated the 'submission of the constitution to the vote of the 'people, as the only course that was safe or proper. 'This is the more important, as Judge Elmore is a 'man of very decided ability, and of great influence 'with the pro-slavery party. He was president of 'this Democratic convention, and is a delegate to 'the constitutional convention which assembles in 'September next. This resolution, which was regarded as substantially against the submission of 'the constitution to the vote of the people, was 'laid on the table as *a test vote*, by a vote of forty-'two to one."

Forty-two to one of this Democratic convention were in favor of submitting the constitution, when it should be framed, to a vote of the people. So you see, sir, that, from the beginning to the end, the free-State men were led to believe, and did believe, that, in any event, this constitution must and would be submitted to the people, or that it would be rejected by Congress. It was admitted on all hands that the convention did not represent the people of Kansas. No man pretended that it represented the people of Kansas; and its members did not pretend it themselves. They only represented a very small fraction of the people of Kansas. Neither does the constitution now upon our table represent the wishes of one in ten of the people of Kansas. The people are opposed to it, and they have resolved, by an emphatic vote of more than ten thousand against it, that they will have nothing to do with it. I trust the attempt may never be made to force them to touch the unclean thing.

The next step in this programme was the election of the Legislature last fall. Again the free-State men were urged and implored by Governor Walker to go to the polls and vote under the code of laws. The more objectionable test oaths were repealed, or decided to be null and void; they were not operative. Through the influence of Governor Walker, and by the advice, I believe, of the Administration here, or of the President and Secretary of State, perhaps, it was decided that those test oaths should not be enforced, and that the people, the *bona fide* residents of Kansas, who had been there three months, should be entitled to vote. Under these pledges, and believing that Governor Walker was sincere and in earnest, and that they would have a fair chance to express their views through the ballot-box, they did go to the polls and vote; they elected their Legislature overwhelmingly; but the moment this was discovered, new returns began to come in, and at last up came a return from Oxford precinct, of Johnson county, with sixteen hundred fraudulent votes attached to that return list; and those sixteen hundred fraudulent votes, if allowed, secured a pro-slavery majority in the Legislature. I am informed that the Cincinnati Directory was copied alphabetically, until they had taken sixteen hundred names, and returned them as having voted at that election—Governor Chase voting the pro-slavery ticket!

When Mr. Walker and Mr. Stanton learned these facts, they said, "we will go down to Johnson county and see whether this can be so." They went down to Johnson county, and brought up a report that there were some six houses in that voting precinct; that there was a small village across the street in Missouri; and they were informed by the people there that not one-tenth of the number returned as having voted there were in the town during the two days the poll books were open. They ascertained that there was not one-tenth of the number on the poll books in the voting precinct; and ascertained that even the Missourians had not come over in those numbers and voted. Not because of the fraud, but because these returns were not put in legal form, the Governor rejected them. He did not claim that he had a right to look into fraudulent returns; but because they were returned to him illegally, he threw them out. Even the provisions of the law under which they were acting were not complied with; and therefore, for that reason, as he informs us, he went behind the record. Up to this time Governor Walker had done everything that had been demanded of him; but for this one honest act, for redeeming this one pledge, Mr. Walker's head was brought to the block. This alone was his unpardonable sin. He had taken the responsibility of throwing out these fraudulent returns, when they had not even the color of law to thrust them in; but for that act, and for that act alone, he was decapitated. After he left the Territory, Secretary Stanton saw fit to call the Legislature together, as he assures us, to prevent civil war or bloodshed, and he, too, lost his place. But before I come to that, I will touch upon the submission of this constitution to the people. Mr. Buchanan, in his special message transmitting the Lecompton constitution, says:

"The question of slavery was submitted to an 'election of the people of Kansas, on the 21st De-'cember last, in obedience to the mandate of the 'constitution. Here again a fair opportunity was 'presented to the adherents of the Topeka con-'stitution, if they were the majority, to decide this 'exciting question 'in their own way,' and thus re-'store peace to the distracted Territory; but they 'again refused to exercise their right of popular 'sovereignty, and again suffered the election to 'pass by default."

* * * * * *

"They now ask admission into the Union under 'this constitution, which is republican in its form. 'It is for Congress to decide whether they will ad-'mit or reject the State which has thus been cre-'ated. For my own part, I am decidedly in favor 'of its admission, and thus terminating the Kansas 'question. This will carry out the great principle 'of non-intervention recognized and sanctioned by 'the organic act, which declares, in express lan-'guage, in favor of 'non-intervention by Congress 'with slavery in the States or Territories,' leaving ''the people thereof perfectly free to form and 'regulate their domestic institutions in their own 'way, subject only to the Constitution of the United 'States.'"

Thus, you see, the President informs us that a fair submission of the slavery clause has been made to the people of Kansas. Now, sir, in the instructions of the President, and in the pledges given by Governor Walker and Secretary Stanton, has there been one word said about submitting the slavery question to the people of Kansas? No, sir; not a word. It was the constitution, and the whole constitution, of Kansas, that was to be submitted to a fair vote of the people. But, suppose I admit, for the sake of argument, that the great important clause was that on the subject of slavery? I acknowledge no such thing, for it was not the only one—still it was a very important matter. But admitting, for the sake of the argument, that was the all-important thing to be submitted, was it fairly done? Was even that clause fairly submitted to a vote of the people? Section nine of the Lecompton schedule provides:

"Any person offering to vote at the aforesaid 'election upon said constitution, shall, if chal-'lenged, take an oath to support the Constitution 'of the United States, and to support this consti-

'tution, under the penalties of perjury under the 'territorial laws."

The voter was required to take an oath to support a constitution which he in his heart meant to subvert the very moment he could obtain power to do so. Would any honest man vote under such a test oath as that? No, sir; no honest man could vote; for there was not a free-State man in that Territory but what utterly abhorred, and would never support, that constitution, if it was in his power to resist it; and yet Mr. Buchanan informs us that this was a fair submission of the slavery clause to the people of Kansas! Let us see whether it was a fair submission of even the slavery clause. In case they voted out the slavery clause itself—"then the article providing for slavery shall be stricken from this constitution by the president of this convention, and slavery shall no longer exist in the State of Kansas, except that the right of property in slaves shall in no manner be interfered with."

So, if they voted out the slavery clause, still the right of property in slaves could not be affected; and there is another provision that any constitutional convention which may meet to amend this constitution shall not interfere with slavery.

There was no submission of the slavery clause; and President Buchanan, if he had read this constitution, must have known it. The right of property in slaves, it was said, shall never be interfered with in this Territory, if they vote out the slavery clause. It was a fraud from beginning to end. I have shown you how these laws were enacted; and now, for fear some of those laws might be repealed, they settle that point in this constitution itself, by declaring:

"All laws now of force in the Territory of 'Kansas which are not repugnant to this constitution, shall continue to be of force until altered, 'amended, or repealed, by a legislature assembled 'under the provisions of this constitution."

It must be remembered that the present Legislature of the Territory of Kansas is a free-State Legislature. The first act, of course, of that free-State Legislature would be to repeal the infamous code; but to perpetuate their power they put into the constitution a bar to any action of the Legislature on that code, and yet any man voting for that constitution swore to support that code, swore that the present free-State Legislature should not alter those laws. There was no submission of the constitution to the people. It was a fraud from the beginning to the end.

Besides, there was no punishment at that time for illegal returns. Mr. Stanton says on this subject:

"I have already expressed the grave doubts I 'entertain as to the power of the Legislature in 'any manner to interfere with the proceedings of 'the convention. But there can be no question 'as to your authority to provide, by a suitable 'law, for a fair expression of the will of the people upon the vital question of approving the 'constitution."

This is in his message to the free-State Legislature. Again he says:

"The laws now prevailing in this Territory provide for the proper punishment of illegal and fraudulent voting, but there is no provision which will 'reach the case of fraudulent returns. The case 'of the late Oxford precinct in Johnson county 'was an enormity so great that it has nowhere 'been defended or justified. Yet the evil consequences of it are seen in the fact that even the 'late convention has been so far imposed upon 'that in its apportionment for the State Legislature, under the constitution, it has assigned to 'Johnson county four representatives, which must 'necessarily be based on the notoriously false returns from that county. In order to meet the 'apprehensions naturally growing out of these 'circumstances, I recommend the adoption of a 'provision making it felony, with suitable punishment, for any judge or clerk of election knowingly to place on the poll books the names of 'persons not actually present and voting, or otherwise corruptly to make false returns, either of 'the election held by order of the convention, or 'of any other election to be held in this Territory."

Here, sir, is what was recommended by Secretary Stanton to the Legislature, to prevent frauds. The constitution was submitted to the people, to a fair vote of the people, under the authority of law, by the present Legislature of Kansas; and it was rejected by the people, by a majority of more than ten thousand votes; while it is proven that at the former submission, on the 21st of December, of the six thousand pro-slavery votes cast, not exceeding two thousand were actual voters in the Territory of Kansas. They were fraudulently made up. We have returns again from Oxford precinct as outrageous as the first. We have almost the whole vote of Johnson county a fraudulent vote; and upon that vote are based four members of the Assembly and one or two of the other branch.

I deny, then, that this constitution has been submitted to the people of Kansas in any proper form but once, and then it was rejected by an overwhelming vote of more than ten thousand. Then the returning of fraudulent votes could be punished. It was made felony. No man dared bring in a fraudulent return, for he would go to prison for so doing; but at the fraudulent election of December 21st, when fraudulent returns might be received, accepted, and counted, it was done.

Complaint was made here the other day, that some of the officers of Kansas had fled for fear of their lives. I should think they would flee for fear of their lives. They have come to the only city of refuge that can afford them any protection. They have committed crimes in Kansas against the law, and if they go there they will be punished according to law, and if they ever get their deserts it will be at the end of a halter. I should think they would dread the Territory of Kansas, and the climate there as unhealthy for their particular complaints.

Mr. President, we have upon our table a very singular document. I do not know what business it has here, but it is here. I should not consider myself entitled to quote from it, or talk about it, if it had not been laid upon our table in an official manner. In accordance with resolutions of the Senate of the 16th and 18th of December last, requiring the President to furnish certain information concerning the government of Kansas, he has transmitted to us a letter from some gentlemen in New Haven and his reply to them. I do not know what business that has here, but being laid on our table I suppose it is a fair subject for comment. In this Senate Document No. 8, at page 74, President Buchanan says:

"Slavery existed at that period and still exists 'in Kansas, under the Constitution of the United 'States. This point has at last been finally decided 'by the highest tribunal known to our laws. How 'it could ever have been seriously doubted is a 'mystery."

How that assertion ever could have been made is to me a mystery. We have very distinguished authority for entertaining doubts. In a letter of Mr. James Buchanan, dated Washington, August 25, 1847, directed to a Harvest Home of the Democracy of Berks county, Pennsylvania, I find this language:

"After Louisiana was acquired from France by 'Mr. Jefferson, and when the State of Missouri, 'which constituted a part of it, was about to be 'admitted into the Union, the Missouri question 'arose, and, in its progress, threatened the dissolu- 'tion of the Union. This was settled by the men 'of the last generation, as other important and 'dangerous questions have been settled, in a spirit 'of mutual concession. Under the Missouri com- 'promise, slavery was 'forever prohibited' north of 'the parallel of 36 degrees 30 minutes: and south 'of this parallel the question was left to be de- 'cided by the people. Congress, in the admission 'of Texas, following in the foot steps of their 'predecessors, adopted the same rule; and, in my 'opinion, the harmony of the States, and even the 'security of the Union itself, require that the line 'of the Missouri compromise should be extended 'to any new territory which we may acquire from 'Mexico."

The James Buchanan who wrote this letter is now astonished that any man should ever doubt that slavery existed in Kansas under the Constitution of the United States! Again, in the same letter, he says:

"Such has been my individual opinion, openly 'and freely expressed, ever since the commence- 'ment of the present unfortunate agitation; and 'of all places in the world, I prefer to put them 'on record before the incorruptible Democracy of 'old Berks. I therefore beg leave to offer you 'the following sentiment:

"*The Missouri Compromise*—Its adoption in '1820 saved the Union from threatened convul- 'sion. Its extension in 1848 to any new territory 'which we may acquire, will secure the like happy 'results."

And that compromise covered the very Territory that he is astonished anybody should ever doubt was covered with slavery! But again, from the same distinguished authority, we find this:

"Having urged the adoption of the Missouri 'compromise, the inference is irresistible that 'Congress, in my opinion, possesses the power to 'legislate upon the subject of slavery in the Ter- 'ritories."

This is the man who is astonished that any one should ever doubt that slavery exists in all the Territories under the Constitution of the United States! It is only ten short years since he wrote the letter; it is less than ten years since he uttered the sentiments I have just quoted.

But I have other distinguished authorities on this very point; among them, the honorable Secretary of State. You see we have had distinguished teachers. We have learned our lessons from high authority, and our doubts are honest. General Cass, in his speech at Romeo, in Michigan, in 1854, said:

"But you cannot put your finger on the power 'thereby ceded to carry slaves into our new Ter- 'ritories. Does the Constitution give authority 'to interefere? No. The word slave is not to be 'found in that instrument."

True.

"There is no power of interference recognized 'by our statute-books except in the case of fugi- 'tives. Go to the Constitution, and if authorized, 'interfere, but otherwise touch not the festering 'evil."

And further, he says:

"Again, it has been said that the passage of 'this bill opens Kansas and Nebraska to the slave 'power. There never was a worse misrepresenta- 'tion."

This is General Cass, the present Secretary of State, who utters that sentiment—"there never was a worse misrepresentation" than that the repeal of the Missouri compromise opened these Territories to slavery:

"Slavery is created by municipal law, and Judge 'McLean says that without law slavery cannot ex- 'ist. The negroes of Kentucky and Pennsylvania 'would alike be free unless slavery had been le- 'galized. How can the master hold slaves with- 'out positive law?"

This is General Cass in 1854. Now, sir, had Mr. Buchanan any reason to utter the sentiment I have read from his letter to the gentlemen from New Haven? I hold that he had not. It was under his teachings and those of his present Secretary of State that I learned the doubt. But again he goes on—I have not done with this letter to New Haven—

"If a confederation of sovereign States acquire 'a new territory at the expense of their common 'blood and treasure, surely one set of the partners 'can have no right to exclude the others from its 'enjoyment, by prohibiting them from taking into 'it whatsoever is recogniz d to be property by the 'common Constitution. But when the people, the '*bona fide* residents of such Territory, proceed to 'frame a State constitution, then it is their right 'to decide the important question for themselves 'whether they will continue, modify, or abolish 'slavery. To them, and to them alone, does this 'question belong, free from all foreign inter- 'ference."

What I have read before of Mr. Buchanan's former views answers that in full, and therefore I shall not comment upon it; but here is what I am coming at:

"I have entire confidence in Governor Walker 'that the troops will not be employed except to 'resist actual aggression or in the execution of 'the laws, and this not until the power of the civil 'magistrate shall prove unavailing. Following the 'wise example of Mr. Madison towards the Hart- 'ford convention"—

Now I am not disposed to take this evidence in regard to the Hartford convention unquestioningly; for it is a well-established principle of law that a man who turns States' evidence must have some confirmatory testimony, or you cannot convict. I am not disposed to take this imputation unless there is some corrobative testimony, and I do not find any; therefore, I do not give any weight to this slur on the Hartford convention or the Topeka convention—

"Illegal and dangerons combinations, such as 'that of the Topeka convention, will not be dis- 'turbed, unles they shall attempt to perform some 'act which will bring them into actual collision 'with the Constitution and the laws. In that 'event they shall be resisted and put down by the 'whole power of the Government. In perform- 'ing this duty, I shall have the approbation of 'my own conscience, and, as I humbly trust, of 'my God."

Mr. President, what laws are these that he is going to use the whole power of the Government to enforce? There was a code of laws enacted in Kansas which the present Secretary of State, General Cass, declared to be a disgrace to the age—a code of laws which the same high authority declared to be unconstitutional, and therefore void. It certainly cannot be those laws which he was going to bring the whole power of the Goverment to enforce. Let us see. Let us see what those laws are that he proposes to bring the whole power of the Government to enforce, and then humbly trusts he will have the approbation of his conscience and his God! In the code of Kansas at page 605, will be found the following enactment."

"SEC. 11. If any person print, write, introduce 'into, publish, or circulate, or cause to be brought 'into, printed, written, published, or circulated, or 'shall knowingly aid or assist in bringing into, 'printing, publishing, or circulating, within the 'Territory, any book, paper, pamphlet, magazine, 'handbill, or circular, containing any statements, 'arguments, opinions, sentiment, doctrine, advice, 'or inuendo, calculated to produce a disorderly, 'dangerous, or rebellious disaffection among the 'slaves in this Territory, or to induce such slaves 'to escape from the service of their masters, or 'to resist their authority, he shall be guilty of 'felony, and be punished by imprisonment and 'hard labor for a term not less than five years."

And yet the Constitution, to which I called your attention a short time since, declares the freedom of speech and of the press shall not be interfered with. This enactment is unconstitutional and void; and yet Mr. Buchanan says, i: the enforcement of this law "all the power of the Government shall be brought into requisition, and in performing this duty I shall have the approbation of my own conscience, and, I humbly trust, of my God," Sir, I do not know of what material his conscience may be made, but there are few men who would have the approbation of their own consciences in that, and there is no attribute in the Divine Being that authorizes any man to say that he humbly trusts he will have the approbation of his God in such an effort.

But again:

"SEC. 12. If any free person, by speaking or 'by writing, assert or maintain that persons have 'not the right to hold slaves in this Territory, 'or shall introduce into this Territory, print, 'publish, write, circulate, or cause to be in- 'troduced into this Territory, written, printed, 'published, or circulated in this Territory, any 'book, paper, magazine, pamphlet, or circular, 'containing any denial of the right of persons to 'hold slaves in this Territory, such person shall 'be deemed guilty of felony, and punished by im- 'prisonment at hard labor for a term of not less 'than two years."

This law he is going to enforce in the same way and have the same approbation! I might go on *ad libitum*, but I shall detain the Senate but a moment on this point. I will read one more law:

"SEC. 4. If any person shall entice, decoy, or 'carry away out of this Territory, any slave be- 'longing to another, with the intent to deprive 'the owner thereof of the services of such slave, 'or with the intent to effect or procure the free- 'dom of such slave, he shall be adjudged guilty of 'grand larcency, and, on conviction thereof, shall 'suffer death, or be imprisoned at hard labor for 'not less than ten years."

For the enforcement of that law all the powers of the Government are to be brougt into requisition, and Mr. Buchanan, in performing this duty, will have the approbation of his own conscience, and, he humbly trusts, of his God. I have done with that New Haven letter. It would have been better if it had never been laid upon our tables, in my estimation.

Mr. Buchanan asserted in his message—I read from page 20 of the first volume of the Message and Documents for this year—

"The friends and supporters of the Nebraska 'and Kansas act, when struggling on a recent oc- 'casion to sustain its wise provisions before the 'great tribunal of the American people, never 'differed about its true meaning on this subject. 'Everywhere throughout the Union they publicly 'pledged their faith and their honor that they 'would cheerfully submit the question of slavery 'to the decision of the *bona fide* people of Kansas, 'without any restriction or qualification whatever. 'All were cordially united upon the great doctrine 'of popular sovereignty, which is the vital princi- 'ple of our free institutions.

"Had it been insinuated from any quarter that 'it would be a sufficient compliance with the re- 'quisitions of the organic law for the members of a 'convention, thereafter to be elected, to withhold 'the question of slavery from the people, and to 'substitute their own will for that of a legally as- 'certained majority of all their constituents, this 'would have been instantly rejected. Everywhere 'they remained true to the resolution adopted on 'a celebrated occasion, recognizing 'the right of 'the people of all the Territories, including Kan- 'sas and Nebraska, acting through the legally and 'fairly expressed will of a majority of actual resi-

'dents, and whenever the number of their inhab- 'itants justifies it, to form a constitution, with or 'without slavery, and be admitted into the Union 'upon terms of perfect equality with the other 'States."

I think that the friends of Mr. Buchanan pledged more than that. I aver that throughout the whole North, the subject of slavery, in that constitution, was never alluded to as the question to be submitted to the people. I aver that pledges were given that the whole constitution should be submitted to the people, and to a fair vote of the people of Kansas. I have shown that there was no submission even of the slavery clause itself; but that was not enough. They pledged more. They pledged Mr. Buchhnan as being favorable to making Kansas a free State; and, in my own State, the embattled hosts of the Democracy marched to defeat under flaunting banners of "Buchanan and free Kansas." In Pennsylvania, I am told, it was the same. Mr. Buchanan was everywhere throughout the North represented as being in favor of making Kansas a free State, and it was asserted over and over again, that the surest way to make it a free State was by the election of James Buchanan. James Buchanan occupies the presidential chair to-day, in consequence of the belief of the people of the North in these fraudulent representations. But for these false assertions he never would have been elected. He never would have carried a single northern State but for the belief in these fraudulent assertions. Now let them carry out their pledges made before the election. Let the constitution be submitted to a fair vote of the people, or else let the whole subject be sent back again to the people to manage their domestic institutions in their own way.

Sir, throughout the North, for many years past, we have had a set of men in great trouble and tribulation about this Union. From every stump in my own State the cry has gone forth, time and again, of "danger to the Union." Throughout all the northern States the same cry has gone forth; and whenever an aggression has been made by the South upon the North, these Union-savers have come before the people, and, in piteous tones, averred that they assented to it to save the Union. That set of people, who have been in labor, and suffering, and trial, for so long a time on account of the Union have passed off the stage. In their places are men who love this glorious Union, and love it as it was made by the fathers; men who will not whine "danger to the Union;" but brave men, who will fight for this Union to the death. The race of Union-whiners, the old women of the North, who have been in the habit of crying out "the Union is in danger," have passed off the stage. They are dead; their places will never be supplied; but in their stead we have a race of men who are devoted to this Union, and devoted to it as Jefferson and the fathers made it and bequeathed it to us.

Any aggression upon the Constitution has been submitted to by the race that have gone off the stage. They were ready to compromise any principle; anything to save the Union. Sir, the men of the present day will compromise nothing. They are Union-loving men; they love all portions of the Union; and they will sacrifice anything but principle to save the Union. They will, however, make no sacrifice of principle—never, never. No more compromises will ever be submitted to to save this Union. If it is worth saving it will be saved; but if you sap and undermine its foundations, if you place it in such a situation that it must topple, what can you expect but the legitimate results of your own action? The only way that we shall ever save the Union and render it as permanent as the everlasting hills, will be by restoring it to the original foundation upon which the fathers placed it. Those are the "mud-sills" that cannot be undermined; and there, sir, this great national Republican party proposes to place it. Sir, we are the national party of the Government, and in opposition to us is a purely sectional party, that knows no issue but one, and that is the slavery issue.

But I am occupying more time than I intended, and I must hasten to a conclusion. One question I wish to propound. I wish to know from some friend of the Lecompton constitution how he proposes to force a State into this Union against the wishes of its government and its people? I wish to know from what clause in the Constitution of the United States you derive the right to force a State into this Union? I assert that should you adopt this constitution for Kansas, you make a dead letter. The government of Kansas, which your own present Executive has admitted to be legal is opposed to this constitution. The people of Kansas are overwhelmingly opposed to it. Now, sir, will some man tell me how, with a government and a people almost unanimously opposed to a constitution, you are going to force it into this Union? The Government of the United States has not bayonets enough, nor money enough to pay for sufficient bayonets, to force a constitution on the necks of any people. It cannot be done. There is no constitutional right to attempt to do it. I respect the President of the United States so long as he obeys and stands by the Constitution of the United States; but let him step one inch beyond that Constitution; let one drop of blood flow in Kansas, or anywhere else, and James Buchanan, President of these United States, will be liable to impeachment, and to be hanged for murder also. James Buchanan, so long as he stays within the Constitution and within the laws, is to be respected by everybody; but let him step beyond the Constitution and beyond the protection of the laws, and he is no longer James Buchanan, President of the United States, but James Buchanan, the criminal. There is no power in this Government to force a constitution on the necks of an unwilling people. It cannot be done. If you adopt the Lecompton constitution to-morrow, you cannot enforce it; it will be a dead letter. Blood may flow—blood will flow, if you attempt to enforce it—but it cannot be enforced.

The honorable Senator from Mississippi [Mr. DAVIS] the other day stated that it was the purpose of the opponents of the Army bill, in civil war, to shed blood on the soil of these United States. I am sorry that Senator is not in his seat; I am sorry that he is unwell, for I intended to comment on this remark. In answer to some observations which I had the honor to submit on the Army bill, he said:

"I do not think the United States Senate can 'fail, under such an argument as has been offered 'by the gentleman who has just taken his seat, to 'see that the opposition springs from the purpose, 'in civil war, of shedding blood on the soil of the 'United States."

The opposition to the Army bill sprung from no such purpose. The opposition to that and to the Lecompton usurpation springs from no such purpose. It is our purpose to avoid the shedding of blood upon the soil of the United States by civil war. While I will not charge on the supporters of the Lecompton constitution the purpose, in civil war, of shedding blood upon the soil of the United States, I do charge that they, and they alone, will be resposible for every drop of blood that may be shed in consequence of the adoption of that constitution. I trust in God civil war will never come; but if it should come, upon their heads, and theirs alone, will rest the responsibility of every drop that may flow. I trust in God, sir, that this question will never be pushed to that extremity, for I should have less respect for the people of Kansas than I now have, if I supposed they would tamely submit to have a constitution thrust down their throats without authority of law, and against law, without their making resistance. I would disown them as the descendants of the men who fought our revolutionary battles, if I did not think they would resist any such illegal attempt to force a constitution upon them. I believe they will resist it if the attempt be made, but I do not believe that the attempt will be made. I trust it will not.

Mr. President, I have occupied more time than I intended, and yet I am not quite through. I shall be as brief as I possibly can, but I desire to allude to some remarks of the honorable Senator from South Carolina, [Mr. HAMMOND.] That Senator said:

"In all social systems there must be a class to 'do the menial duties, to perform the drudgery of 'life. That is, a class requiring but a low order of 'intellect, and but little skill. Its requisites are 'vigor, docility, fidelity. Such a class you must 'have, or you would not have that other class 'which leads progress, civilization, and refinement. 'It constitutes the very mud-sill of society and of 'political government; and you might as well attempt to build a house in the air, as to build either 'the one or the other, except on this mud-sill. 'Fortunately for the South, she found a race adapt'ed to that purpose to her hand. A race inferior 'to her own, but eminently qualified in temper, in 'vigor, in docility, in capacity to stand the climate, 'to answer all her purposes. We use them for our 'purpose, and call them slaves. We found them 'slaves by the 'common consent of mankind,' 'which, according to Cicero, '*lex naturæ est*.' The 'highest proof of what is Nature's law. We are 'old-fashioned at the South yet; it is a word dis'carded now by 'ears polite;' I will not character'ize that class at the North with that term; but 'you have it; it is there; it is everywhere; it is 'eternal.

"The Senator from New York said yesterday 'that the whole world had abolished slavery. Ay, 'the *name*, but not the *thing;* all the Powers of 'the earth cannot abolish that. God only can do 'it when he repeals the *fiat*, 'the poor ye always 'have with you;' for the man who lives by daily 'labor, and scarcely lives at that, and who has to 'put out his labor in the market, and take the best 'he can get for it; in short, your whole hireling 'class of manual laborers and 'operatives,' as you 'call them, are essentially slaves. The difference 'between us is, that our slaves are hired for life 'and well compensated; there is no starvation, no 'begging, no want of employment among our 'people, and not too much employment either. 'Yours are hired by the day, not cared for, and 'scantily compensated, which may be proved in 'the most painful manner, at any hour, in any 'street in any of your large towns."

After reading and reperusing that speech, I proceeded to consider the state of society where such a happy population was found; and I began to examine into the condition of the people of South Carolina. I am not in the habit of saying, and I will not now say, one word to disparage any State, or the people of any State, in this Union; but I think that attack requires a reply; and I shall read from some distingushed southern authorities in elucidation of this statement. I find in an address of a late Chief Magistrate of South Carolina, Governor Hammond, before the South Carolina Institute, the following exposition:

"According to the best calculations which, in 'the absence of statistic facts, can be made, it is 'believed that, of the three hundred thousand '*white* inhabitants of South Carolina, there are not 'less than fifty thousand whose industry, such as 'it is, is not, in the present condition of things, 'and does not promise, hereafter, to b , adequate 'to procure them, honestly, such a support as 'every white person in this country is, and feels 'himself entitled to.

"Some cannot be said to work at all. They 'obtain a precarious subsistence by occasional jobs, 'by hunting, by fishing, sometimes by plundering 'fields or folds, and too often, by what is, in its 'effects, far worse—trading with slaves, and se'ducing them to plunder for their benefit."

Fifty thousand out of three hundred thousand, I am told by this authority, are in that condition in the State of South Carolina. I find other high authority upon this same question. Mr. De Bow, in his Review, says:

"It is too obvious to require extended illustra'tion, that the slow advance of our population 'mainly arises from the impoverished condition of 'our lands. As lands become exhausted the re'turns are not only small and unremunerating, 'but crops become uncertain, from casualities and 'vicissitudes of season, subsistence more precari'ous, and obtained at greater cost. The striking 'fact that those districts possessing naturally the 'best soils are almost stationary in population, 'while districts of inferior soils naturally are fill'ing up, show not only the exhausted state of the 'soil in the former, but prove that the character 'of slave labor, and the system of cultivation 'adopted, are unfriendly to density of population.

"The exhaustion of our lands, above alluded to, 'is further evinced by the fact that, in the last 'thirty years, they have remained generally sta'tionary in price; and, in many instances, have 'actually declined. Another fact, very significant 'of this truth, is the regularly increased amount 'of lands cultivated in different crops per hand, 'particularly in cotton, while the amount pro-'duced is proportionably less."

And again, the business committee of the South Carolina Agricultural Society reported, August 9, 1855:

"Our old fields are enlarging, our homesteads 'have been decreasing fearfully in number.,' * * '"We are not only losing some of our most en-'ergetic and useful citizens to supply the bone 'and sinew of other States, but we are losing our 'slave population, which is the true wealth of the 'State; our stocks of hogs, horses, mules, and 'cattle, are diminishing in size and decreasing in 'number; and our purses are strained for the last 'cent to supply their places from the nortwestern 'States."

That is not so flattering an account as I hope to give of Michigan by-and-by. In the message of Governor Seabrook, of South Carolina, to the Legislature, I find:

"Education has been provided by the Legisla-'ture but for one class of the citizens of the State, 'which is the wealthy class. For the middle and 'poorer classes of society it has done nothing, 'since no organized system has been adopted for 'that purpose. You have appropriated $75,000 'annually to the free schools; but, under your 'present mode of applying it, that liberality is 'really the profusion of the prodigal, rather than 'the judicious generosity which confers real bene-'fit. The few who are educated at public expense 'in these excellent and truly useful institutions, 'the Arsenal and Citadel academies [military 'schools] form almost the only exception to the 'truth of this remark. Ten years ago, twenty 'thousand adults, besides children, were unable to 'read or write, in South Carolina. Has our free 'school system dispelled any of this ignorance? 'Are there not any reasonable fears to be enter-'tained that the number has increased since that 'period?"

Again, writes a distinguished traveller of the "sand-hillers" of Sonth Carolina:

"Not very essentially different is the condition 'of a class of people living in the pine-barrens 'nearest the coast, as described to me by a rice-'planter. They seldom have any meat, he said, 'except they steal hogs which belong to the plan-'ters or their negroes, and their chief diet is rice 'and milk. They are small, gaunt, and cadaver-'ous, and their skin is just the color of the sand-'hills they live on. They are quite incapable of 'applying themselves steadily to any labor, and 'their habits are very much like those of the old 'Indians.

"A northern gentleman, who had been spend-'ing a year in South Carolina, said to me, after 'speaking respectfully of the character of some of 'the wealthier class, 'but the poor whites, out in 'the country, are the meanest people I ever saw: 'half of them would be considered objects of 'charity in New York."

The picture is not so flattering when you come to examine it closely. It is one of those beautiful paintings where "distance lends enchantment to the view." I should not have alluded to this subject but for the attack of the honorable Senator upon my constituents, the laborers of the North. Sir, under his version, under his exposition of slavery, nine tenths of the people of the North are, or have been at some period of their lives, slaves; for nine tenths of the people of the North have, at some time, been hireling laborers. We do not feel degraded by being hireling laborers. We believe it to be respectable. You may travel on any road in the State of Michigan you see fit to select, and you will find flourishing farms on almost every one hundred and sixty acres—nice farm houses, comfortable dwellings, fine barns, a very high state of improvement and cultivation; and you do not find the fifty thousand class that you find in South Carolina. Sir, we deny that the laboring men of the North are, or can be, construed into slaves. They are men. These very laboring men are the foundations of society there. Go through the agricultural portion of Michigan, and you will find the farmer with four or five of the sons of his neighboring farmers employed as hirelings by the day, by the month, or by the year. A young man goes out to service—to labor, if you please to call it so—for compensation until he acquires money enough to buy a farm, and then he gets married and settles upon his farm, and anon he becomes himself the employer of labor. He never feels himself degraded by his labor. Some of those men who are at work by the month, during the summer, on farms, are in the Legislature making laws for us in the winter.

We have an eminent example of the class of which the Senator from South Carolina terms slaves. The late Speaker of the House of Representatives of the United States, Mr. Banks, now the Governor of Massachusetts, only fifteen years ago was working by the day, for his support, in a machine-shop. Fifteen years afterwards you find him occupying certainly the third place within the gift of the people of this nation; ten years hence, and you may see him in the executive chair. He never deemed himself degraded by the labor that he performed in that machine-shop; nor do our men admit that there is degradation in such employment.

But, sir, I have already occupied too much time. I have hurriedly passed over topics which I could have desired more time to discuss. They teem with interest and instruction. Nevertheless, with thanks to the Senate for the courteous attention with which it has heard me, I yield the floor.

www.ingramcontent.com/pod-product-compliance
Lightning Source LLC
LaVergne TN
LVHW011146110826
845150LV00008B/2535
9781418191870